Bernice is a new author who has just entered the world of writing. After years of searching for her passion, she finally found that she must share her gift with others of how she makes it in life- the good, the bad and the ugly. The middle child to a total of 5 siblings, Bernice was doing everything right; job after high school, went to college, received several degrees but, despite it all, was still in search of her passion. It was evident to Bernice that she wanted to help and be of service to people. Not finding her passion within her chosen career path. Bernice decided to help through these written words to help others better understand how they can help themselves.

May this book bring you Positivity, clarity, and guidance!

Bernice

Table of Contents

The Weight

God has repeatedly brought me through- he has helped me get to where I am and where I plan to go in life. While you may or may not be religious, please know that my life's journey, which has birthed the words in this book, was guided by a higher power. Each day I strive to be a better me, and I have taken the steps necessary to focus on my growth and development. I am now able to reap the benefits of that work and wish to share my lessons with you.

It is so difficult being an adult, especially when you face countless obstacles that hinder your progression. While going through this thing called life with family, friends, your career, and your significant other, it can be hard to maintain focus. LET'S BE REAL: Some days it can even be difficult to get out of bed.

The Weight

In this book, I give advice on how to be the best person that you can be by moving in positivity and focusing on self. Each chapter identifies things you may witness in your daily life and/or find yourself doing to others. Each page will provide nuggets of information to help you move through life's circumstances in positivity while focusing on **self-development and self-reflection**.

This book will also address how to steer clear of people who deter you from being your greatest and most productive self.

I believe that experience is the best teacher and my journey has taken me through many experiences. There was a time when I saw the negative in every situation. I would pray often and realized that what I prayed for in life, I never obtained. It was so confusing and always left me asking "Why?" After a while, I realized that my outlook was to blame. I had to ask myself, "How can you be positive and bring light into your life if you dwell in the negative? How can good things ever come into your life?"

Eventually, I admitted that whenever good things came to me, I often found a way to engulf those things in negativity.

So, the question in all of this is- how did I stop my constant consumption of negativity? I first decided to change my mindset and began to think positively about every aspect of my life. If I encountered an obstacle, I decided (**Hint:** DECIDED) to be positive and visualize the outcome would be in my favor. In every situation, you choose how you feel about it and what your reaction to it will be. It is your choice to be either negative or positive about the situation and the outcome. I decided to identify each of my problems and work on that shit until something changed. And it did.

The proof is in the pudding.

Also, I decided to surround myself with those who possessed and exhibited the positive energy that I wanted in my life. Think about it- if you are trying to be your best self, how can you continue to be surrounded by those who are not doing the same? Ultimately, you will find yourself working to uplift them and make them happy. You will be unable to adequately focus on self and the things that you wish to accomplish in your life. People who dwell in negative spaces can be unintentionally draining and unfavorable to your progression. It is not always necessary to completely remove these people from your

The Weight

life as some may be your friends, family members or
even your partner. However, for your personal growth
and development, you should separate yourself enough
to ensure that you do not become engrossed in their
negativity.

Why take on the baggage of others or surround
yourself with those who wish to unload their baggage
on you?

BE YOU

One day, I sat in a room and looked around. I noticed that I was the only one there- and it was at this point that I realized it was time to be me. To be "me" I had to pull from deep within. It was in this space that I was also able to see a glimpse of the "me" seen by others.

I didn't like it.

They didn't like it.

I couldn't fake it anymore; It was time to change and officially accept being "me."

The Weight

"Be You" is such a simple statement but holds a strong meaning. It is imperative that we determine what it means to "Be You." To figure this out, start by asking whether you spend time attempting to live life as someone else or compare your life to the experiences of others.

Don't worry! We all do this to some extent. We look at television and see models and TV personalities who have what we think is better skin, better clothes, a better attitude, and everything better than what we have. For some, this interest in others is consuming. We can become so interested in wanting the perceived lives, accomplishments, and belongings of others without any idea of what that person may have gone through to get what they have. We don't know their story, nor do we care to know. We only see the superficial. When I say, "Be You," I mean exactly that- just be yourself, be real with yourself, acknowledge shit you need to work on to be a better person and put in the effort to change. Don't worry about the lives of other people. Life is too short for that.

Often, we find it difficult to get our personal lives together because we are so focused on the lives of others. Why do we do this? From my experience, it seems many people believe that when things are going wrong in their lives, the complete opposite is happening to those around them.

In public settings, people often choose to accentuate the positive in their lives which could make those dealing with tough times have a skewed sense of reality. They may compare their difficulty to the perceived perfection in the life of someone else. This is a notably unhealthy mindset to have. If you are always focused on other people and not self, I can guarantee that you will not get very far in your personal development. You will become so fixated with everyone else that you will be unable to focus on how to move forward in life. When going through tricky situations, the best thing you can do is direct your thoughts to your personal circumstances only. When you focus on other people and romanticize their lives, it will do nothing but put you in a mentally unstable space while cluttering your mind with unnecessary thoughts.

Instead of focusing on others, take the time to identify the good in your life. What have you accomplished? What are your talents? What progress have you made in the past year? When you question yourself in this manner, your answers should reassure you that despite what is going on now, you are accomplishing things in your life. You are moving forward. This method of questioning self about achievements is one of the easiest ways to turn negative thoughts positive. Take it one day at a time. Even if all you've done for the day is get out of bed, acknowledge the effort and energy that it took to accomplish that feat. In this sense, you are maintaining a focus on self.

The one thing I always remember when I am feeling down is that I am not the only one with issues. Whether they be mental, physical or emotional, we all carry insecurities and should be working on personal development When I feel myself drifting to the thoughts of someone else's life or my personal difficulties, I immediately switch gears and think about all my accomplishments, how far I've come and where I see myself going in the future. Should this happen to you, refocus your mind and get back to what is most important- YOU! Soon you will realize that you are the center of your universe. If you are the best that you can be, everything around you, including your perceptions, relationships, and way of life will reflect appropriately.

Focusing on yourself takes a lot of effort; you must spend a significant amount of time alone, thinking about the things you need to do to better yourself. To keep your thoughts in order and to track your progress, I suggest that you keep a daily journal. For those who find it difficult to devote time to writing in a traditional journal, feel free to use the memo pad on your phone or tablet. It doesn't matter where you write, all that matters is that you release and keep track of your thoughts. Express how you feel, what you have and ultimately wish to accomplish, as well as anything else that you desire to write. It worked for me.

For months I would take myself to breakfast and write down my thoughts, my desires, my needs, my wants, etc. I focused on my personal development in my career, finances, and overall personal growth. This process was not always pleasant, and I sometimes fought against my own realities. We often like to work out issues with the help of others, which can in some cases, be necessary. As necessary as it may be at times, working through your issues with others (such as a therapist, friend, family member, etc.) is no excuse for wanting people around you to pity your situation. Just as you have issues to work through, so do others. It is never fair or appropriate to expect someone else to pity you. For this reason, working on self first by doing something as simple as journaling, is often a clever idea. In this sense, we can prevent ourselves from channeling someone else's energy into our own. When we take on the energy and perspective of others without a strong personal foundation, we gain a false sense of reality and drain the person from whom we seek help.

Just as you deserve the right to cultivate positivity in your life without carrying the negative baggage of others, those in your circle deserve the same. Don't suck the positive energy out of someone else for personal gain. What do I mean by that? Do not place yourself around someone who embodies positivity so that you take their energy and leave them to bear your baggage. Ultimately, your focus should always remain on self. Other than during your self-assessments, this journey has very little to do with anyone else. In the end, you may find your interactions with others improve, but while traveling this journey, your focus should not be on others- it should be on you.

I have found myself on both ends of the spectrum- I have been the giver and receiver of negativity. I once had a friend that I would call every time I had a problem. I would talk about my issues, never allowing her to speak. It was almost as if I used her as the dumping ground for MY issues. After a while, I noticed that she started to limit our conversations. She stopped answering my calls. I realized quickly that I was extremely selfish, and I completely understood why she no longer wanted to speak to me. I drained her! As a friend, she was there for me initially, but soon she determined that our conversations were unhealthy.

The Weight

She took all that she could from me and had no more to give. I understood.

Our friends are there for companionship and dialogue, so it is unrealistic to think that we should hide all our problems from them. Keep in mind your friend is not your board-certified therapist!

In friendships, we must ride a fine line and make sure that we are balanced and healthy in our interactions. It is also important to note that while working on self, one should be weary of having an excessive number of people active in their inner circle. Since the focus is on self, it is easier to achieve results with fewer people around.

PUT YOURSELF FIRST

You've given so much of yourself to others that you

failed to tend to your own needs.

Now, who will help you?

You've given all you had; now you are helpless.

Limit Your Helping Hand

We all feel good when we do for others. The joy that we feel when we know that we've made a difference in someone's life is beautiful. We enjoy this feeling and, as humans, we should always want to help our fellow man. However, it is imperative that when helping others, we never lose sight of our personal needs.

Why do you think a person would be willing to help others but not help themselves? From a personal perspective, what does it mean if you are one who is always looking to give to others while neglecting your own needs? What are you trying to avoid by putting all your energy in outside sources rather than self? If you are one who does this, answering these questions are essential to your self-development. If you are unable or just not ready to provide answers, I will give you an idea of why you may be this person who is willing to help everyone else but yourself.

It is possible that you are addicted to the euphoric feeling that comes from knowing that your efforts encouraged change in someone else's life. It is also possible that the only way for you to block out personal issues is to focus on someone or something else.

Addiction to the feeling of helping others can easily turn into utilizing someone else's trials to make yourself feel good. In a sense, looking at someone else as being in a "worse" situation than you and using that to feel good is unhealthy. The hardships of others should not dictate your self-assurance. This is not the proper way to help others. We should provide aid from the goodness of our hearts, not because it will make us feel good inside or because of praise or a reward. If you help someone and become satisfied within because, despite your assistance and their improvements, they are not doing better than you, then what happens when they continue to improve and possibly enter a better position than you? Ultimately, you remain in the same space; your personal life is no better and may be worse than when you started. When giving unto others, the universe will put everything into perspective for you- if your efforts are for good reasons good will come to you.

If you're not, well you know the rest.

Blocking out personal issues by focusing on others is another unhealthy practice that will ultimately leave you unfulfilled. We cannot run away from that which is in ourselves. We may block it for a while, but it never leaves, and at some point, we will have to deal with it.

The Weight

When we attempt to hide from our issues while assisting others, we must also be weary of that superiority feeling that can come with knowing that we are serving others who in many cases, cannot serve themselves. For some, this feeling becomes an excuse to continue focusing on others and not self. Ask yourself- Am I helping others so that I can receive praise? If so, why? This feeling is dangerous and takes the sincerity out of the help provided. It also does nothing for self-development because, after the praise, your issues still exist and must be addressed. Ultimately, it is dangerous to help other people simply because you don't want to think about self. These actions will not make your problems go away. Trust me, I know it's hard. I have been there before. There was a point when I decided that I would focus on helping others while neglecting self so that my problems would disappear. Then I started thinking perhaps God will see me doing good for others and bless my situation. My plan was to leave it in God's hands. That plan never worked. My problems remained (just as yours will) until I decided to resolve them.

You cannot afford not to live a happy life. Live your life, be open to new things, work through your issues and move on.

Each day, remind yourself that you are in control and that you CHOOSE to progress in positivity.

GET RID OF THE NEGATIVITY

When negativity surrounds you, there is limited space for positivity. Be honest with yourself; what kind of energy do you attract & why?

The Weight

Life has its ups and downs. So, it is expected that we all will have good days and bad days. We will have days where we feel on top of the world and other days where we feel like the world is on our shoulders. It is not easy to adopt a positive way of thinking when things are not going our way. While our feelings may vary from day to day, it is always important to be careful of imbalance. We cannot dwell in constant negativity. When we do this, we become consumed - we start to become the negative energy that we experience. This negative energy will affect our attitude, relationships and ability to be successful.

You do not want to be the person that no one wants to be around because of unnecessary negative energy.

You cannot live each day in a negative and depressed state. If you regularly do not want to get out of bed, prefer not to be around people and lack ambition to do anything, then it's time for you to see a therapist or counselor. You MUST obtain professional help if you feel this way every day of your life. When negativity becomes an integral part of your existence, you have essentially become lifeless. This is not living! As I have said many times in this book if negative thoughts consume you, combat them with positivity.

Go to your "happy place" and stay there! As easy as I may make this sound, in practice I do understand that it is very challenging. For some, it is nearly impossible. Therefore, it is important to know when to seek professional help. If you are unable to find that "happy place" regardless of how hard you try, professional help is likely needed. But remember, you are strong, and you are capable. Try to help yourself when you can because, in the end, even when you seek help, you are the one who will make the ultimate difference in your life.

As you move through each day, you will notice people who are genuinely happy and those who are not. You will be able to tell who can turn negative into positive and those who prefer to dwell in negativity. Sometimes seeing attributes in others can help us identify our own character traits. We have all heard the term "misery (negativity) loves company, " and while that may be true, very few people want to be in the company of misery. Therefore, if you prefer to relish in negative thoughts, you may begin to see a decline in the people who choose to be around you.

I will admit that it is hard to change. There is no switch to flip that will turn negativity on and off. However, through dedication, you can alter the way you think. You could identify negative thoughts and choose to replace them with positive thoughts. You can make that decision. Of course, if you ever find it too difficult to transform those thoughts, you may need professional assistance. If this is the case, do not feel bad! Get the help that you need. Ultimately, even if you do require outside help, it will always be your decision to change.

One way to modify negative thought processes is to listen to positive affirmations each day. When I started this practice, it changed my life drastically! Hearing positive words and affirming positivity in my life was a game-changer. While I may not have changed overnight, each day I could see the improvement that eventually resulted in a complete mental transformation. While on this course, I remained

The Weight

honest with myself and never tried to act like I was in a

positive state when I wasn't. I knew that people in my

circle would be able to recognize my energy. Instead, I

decided to accept my journey and work through each of

my evolutions.

<u>LOVE YOURSELF</u>

Before I can feel love, I need to love myself first.

The Weight

It takes a lot of strength to look at yourself in the mirror and say – I love myself - flaws and all. Trust me I know. There were many things that I did not like about myself and still struggle with today. But, to maintain positivity in my life, I strive to release those thoughts that make me self-conscious and uneasy. Life is too short to harp on what you dislike about yourself. I used to look at other people and wish I had what they had, whether it be in their physical appearance or personal belongings.

Then I realized if I was supposed to have what they had, I would have it. And if I am supposed to have it in the future, it will come to me.

In today's world, physical appearance is such a huge concern, to the point where plastic surgery is normalized. People do not have to accept their natural appearance because anything that they do not like can change. This makes it difficult for the average person, one who would likely not have access to or the finances for plastic surgery, to accept themselves as God created them to be. But, to maintain positivity and a level of mental sanity, you must look at yourself in the mirror and realize that all you have is you - physical flaws, imperfections and all. As with anything, this change in thought does not happen overnight. It takes time. For some even years. No matter how long it takes, please know that it is possible to say, "I LOVE ME." If you have not reached this point, do not worry. It takes time, and you are worth every minute, every hour and every day that it takes to change.

It is also essential to note that you must love yourself before you can adequately accept love from others. Just about everyone wants to be loved. We want companionship, a soulmate, spouse, significant other - someone who we can give love and who can provide us love in return. To obtain this love, we must first love ourselves. There will be no need to look for it; the love will come freely. If you search for this love before you are ready to accept it, what you find will be counter-intuitive to your self-development progress. If you are dealing with failed relationships, it is possible that you need to step back and complete more self-work before building new relationships.

Self- love is key to the development of strong relationships with others.

THINK AHEAD

Focusing on the present made me depressed but overcoming the present allowed me to rest!

The Weight

When you feel like things aren't going your way and everything is wrong in your life, what do you do? Some people decide to ignore anything positive and focus solely on the problems that they encounter. When multiple problems hit you at once, it is easy to forget that positivity can be found somewhere in the situation. When it seems like things are a bit much to bear, I try to think ahead. I remember the saying "This too shall pass" and remember that there is a future ahead. Change is constant, what is at this moment will not necessarily be the next. Remember there is no need to sit in bullshit. Always keep it moving.

If you happen to find yourself in this space, start thinking about two weeks from now, maybe even three months from now. Think about the future, a time where your current situation may no longer be your reality.

The Weight

Simply put, focus on a time beyond your current situation. Time stands still for no one, so if there is one thing that is for certain, it is that the future will come, and your present will be the past.

While thinking ahead, consider your current situation and what you can do differently in that inevitable future to ensure that your current situation is never again a reality. Keep your thoughts positive and happy; try to remain in control of your emotional state. Sometimes you may feel comfortable in sorrow but trust me, joy, positivity, and happiness will always make you feel better than any negative emotion ever could.

Living in an unhappy state isn't healthy for you or anyone else!

GET REAL

I can no longer lie

I felt so dead inside

I focused on the wrong

I didn't have room for right

I wanted to sit in my own stuff

No help; just pity

Just sit

I had to find a place

I had to come to grips with things

I had to get real about my stuff

The Weight

If you want to move beyond the obstacles in life and become a better person, you must be real with yourself. There is no need to pretend to be happy when you aren't. Lying to yourself is a quick and effortless way to fall into a depression.

You must be real with yourself to ensure that you provide self with the help and tools necessary to change.

How can you grow and be a better you if you can't be honest with self? The first step is always to admit that there is a problem. From there, you can work on that issue, utilizing whatever tactics necessary for improvement. I can understand why one would choose to be dishonest with themselves. It is hard to admit, even to yourself, that you have a problem that needs to be solved, but dishonesty will only make matters worse.

If your dishonesty is being used to not only appease your ego but also as a display for someone else, you may have an even bigger problem at hand. First, you have yourself to consider. Second, you have the opinions and thoughts of others lagging on to you like unnecessary baggage. People can tell when you are not sincere. You KNOW when you are not sincere (whether you want to admit it to yourself or not). So, in many cases, your dishonest efforts are for naught. I learned long ago not to concern myself with others and just focus on being the best person possible. I reached a point where I no longer cared what others thought of me. My focus was what I thought of myself. What I learned is that I must be true to myself, just as you must be true to yourself, to live a positive and fulfilling life.

The Weight

Staying positive and living the best life possible is easier said than done, trust me, I know. Hence the reason why I wrote this book. However, if you want to get through difficulties, you must focus on self before anyone else. No need to walk around feeling sorry for yourself or expecting others to feel sorry for you. Take the time to get to know yourself, to love yourself and to simply be one with self.

Concerning relationships, you must release negativity and develop a loving connection with self before you can experience strong relationships in your life. As I said, I know this is difficult, but with dedication, you can accomplish anything. I took the time to follow the steps outlined in this book and I am now in a great, fulfilling space. When you radiate positivity, you will notice that positivity is just about the only thing that you will receive in return.

For the steps in this book to work, you must want to change. You can't just talk about it; you must be about it. I put in a lot of work - I prayed a lot, wrote down my goals, and FOCUSED on change. I did everything that I set out to do because I wanted a change in my life. You can do the same.

Use the tools in this book to identify the problems and follow the given suggestions to make a change. Over time, you will see yourself differently and others will too.

Be proud of yourself and what you have accomplished. Be kind to people. Acknowledge the fact you want to change, know there is a light at the end of the tunnel.

The Weight

Release the weight of life from yourself!

Be great!

REMEMBER: You are responsible for your happiness;

only YOU can put in the work to remove the weight!

Made in the USA
Columbia, SC
18 April 2018